SUNDROPS AND LANTERNS: COLLECTED POEMS

William Buck

Antique Geometry & The New Gelatin Press

Also by William Buck
Relic Of Peril: A Novel
The Mermaids & Other Stories

Printed in the United States

Come to me from Crete to this holy temple,
Aphrodite. Here is a grove of apple
trees for your delight, and the smoking altars
　　　　fragrant with incense.

Here cold water rustles down through the apple
branches; all the lawn is beset and darkened
under roses, and, from the leaves that tremble,
　　　　sleep of enchantment

comes descending. Here is a meadow pasture
where the horses graze and with flowers of springtime
now in blossom, here where the light winds passing
　　　　blow in their freshness.

Here in this place, lady of Cypress, lightly
lifting, lightly pour in the golden goblets
as for those who keep a festival, nectar:
　　　　wine for our drinking.

Sappho Of Mytilene

Contents

Heliotrope:

Evening's Shadow:

Heliotrope

Passing Through

Threading the eye of a thoroughfare
close to the trailing yellow meridian

that follows the roll of hills, cracked and cobbled,
bordered by sidewalks like the streets of Laredo,

patchy, with boiled tar and black weeds,
winding through the painted hexagonal

intersections of pocked mortar,
chipped enamels of rainbow mold,

paint streaked layers of yesteryears:
winter, spring, and very hot summers,

young girls in the shadows of cathedrals,
almond eyed, white shirts and braided hair;

arrow headed spikes topping the iron bars
enclosing the Virgin and a winking candle:

rose ash, copper flames, and a well fingered rosary,
automobiles scattered like fallen dogwood,

some on concrete blocks, out-bored, cylindrical,
black oil opalescent beneath the differentials

staining a torn bandanna; the backyards of adobes
surrounded by pepper grass and a chain link fence,

tattered billboards bleeding faded messages,
the promised land in three easy payments:

diets of tequila and salsa, yellow coronas
littering the table tops like bowling pins;

young goats basting in smoky windows,
clouds of pumice settling in doorways,

a steady haze from summer brush fires,
tangled nests of mesquite; wicker baskets

with hand painted eggs, water colored,
on the city's east side, past the interstate,

where sparrows spin a cloth of air
and dive, attending to the sky.

Chameleons

Ramshackle of a barn house leans
murmuring, eaves among caterpillars,

warm rain and a tangle of weeds,
a lattice work covering over

lavender, gold with a tint of blue,
a sudden flash of pink, chartreuse.

Peeping from the cushioning flowers,
pinwheel mandalas on the grassy floor

scatter, then freeze, then form again
tails twitching in brush stroke colors.

Throat puffing quatrefoils, crystalline,
darting and nudging, rapidly advancing:

they are chameleons, colors changing.
What they touch, they become.

Perceiving, they become. Perceive,
absorb or distinguish, nakedly

among the leaves, the old barn
is slowly disappearing. Chameleons appear

like water over stones, or clouds
that rise or dissolve, cold rains

encourage the dalliance. Tongues
forked to changes in the atmosphere,

drops of sunlight on a color wheel.
Tenants of the dreaming green.

Atlantis

Bloom of rhododendron
among the greenwood, antique
omen of the miraculous

conceals my axe handle
lost one morning in a tangle
of shrubs, in a thicket

now lit with wildflowers
brighter than the crowns
    of Atlantis.

That dreaming city,
an island of existing blue
and preeminent

(a mountain daguerreotype
of contrasting greys,
        sharp angled precision
       where ancient civilizations
        rise and vanish;

a cloud of drifting monarchs
over cotton suspended,
       pollen purpled and yellow,
        delicate as cornflowers,
         thin winged)

is as shapely as this bucket
emptied and rusted out
amid leaves of another season.

Jade Terrace

Dispensed, like some mysterious Stone Age manna,
red blocks of granite rest in sempiternal heaps,
blasted out of the sunken quarry by compression's
              ground zero phenomena,

slowly filling in now, as anything gapped will do,
with rippling pools of rainwater, hidden streams
merging and collecting into rich currents of sediment,
              the nourishment of stasis

that creates what is lush, creates life. The oval homes
of orchids, bells of star shaped tendrils, tasseled panicles;
flowers of all colors, but in particular the underlying
              nest of a green so pure

that it seems almost an emerald armor, inching back
toward the sky, a supplicant, a sacrifice climbing steps
on the ridge of a savage temple (or wilderness high-rise);
              the toppled mélange of natural

forms providing a terrace, a purchase, footholds,
the ramparts of a breathing jade landscape flowering
outward like the scrolls of a gerrymandering text,
              a sun selected
                        jeweled
                        crescendo.

Ornamental

∞ December

Our cloven hooves leap from trap to trap,
fire cracks in the skull's attic.
Wings attack, hurtling horns
swirl in the space of my skeleton purse.

In December, sundrops and lanterns
burnish the blossom's color
and the starlit green mesquite dripping
snow and the sharp moon

covering the steps in tinsel, hanging
Christmas on the chimney *lickety split,*
where hearts, amulets, bones and beads
as crystallized tokens, dream.

† Nativity

Nazarene,
poinsettias and angels,
savior of lilac and hillside,
turning to wine, turning

in a manger. White lilies
and a music box. Robes,
red myrtle and thorns
clothe him.

Bright, the emblems

in candlelight and brass
under the crowns
of long stemmed Bethlehem.

Pear Flower

Once as I leaned dreaming
over an edge of prickly pears,
lips purpled and dry, eyes wide,
a pale star said to me:

"The planets which revolve in isolation
are no different from your reflection
in the glass of that wine bottle."

Nodding to the cactus bed, I heard
a nettled green of thorns covered
with opalescent dew drops laughing.
And a pear flower said to me:

"Your mind has become a soft jewel
filled with green fire.
Your heart is written in runes.
Your truths separate from you
like clouds from the ocean,
like leaves from the trees."

It was then that I knew
when on rare occasion
a woman, a friend says to me:

"I think about you all of the time
because I never see you."

That the bats have already flown south,
that the last glass of wine has been poured

(always the last and always the best),
that my thoughts have drifted to Paris, or whether
the coffee's ready.

Spoon

A star drifts in the moon's half cup
as he skirts a weeded tuft where crushed
clovers tend to the frivolous violets.

His memory, a sort of memento moiré
of better days, masquerades as a violet
there, or perhaps clover, or as half a cup.

His ambivalence could be cured, he thinks,
by this walking, or corn on the cob, or a roll
in the sack, or by what he lacks, or a promenade.

He's puzzled about rolls. He's rolling right along
himself, though utterly alone. He knows
he needs some stitch work, feeling spare,

threadbare ... he needs some lacing up.
But what seamstress, from what loom,
could make him smooth and seamless
            as a spoon?

On Holiday

Day 1: The Vase

> Been teasing plum trinkets
> from the tomb of Eurydice,
> where the totemic sprawl
>
> of idols in a brass pot,
> of a tree (bearing apricots),
> of a son of man, of cherries,
>
> engrave a vase. Their sequined trace
> like Thracian snakes *dilates*.
>
> Then a glance to the mirror where
> some euphemistic word, say
> "ad hoc"
>
> entertains a breaking notion
> and labels something silver
> and presents the open question:
> what is your calamity?

Day 2: The Nymphs

> Nymphs in tourmalines
> brisk the shimmering water
> in xylophone silver, damp hair
> and bodies brightly bubbled,
> floating on the cold spray,
> dancing on white sands.

Besparkled in shells,
on blue dolphins carried
to lush islands of eunuchs
whom they chase, scattering
into the banana plants
drunk on burgundy.

Conditions

Pricing desire's trinkets, conditions
bracket epiphanies, distinguish possibilities,
haggle for existences. Conditions are Aztec

bookends of green malachite, fifty percent off
for a short time only; conditions ain't phony:
defining hazards, dressing up backwards,

repelling heaven's icons, putting the ice on.
Can't know it if it's not, so
conditions grow
by declaring things imports, demanding tolls.

Have conditions ever met a thing they didn't like?
If so, how would we know?
Conditions wag the finger, glance askance
at uppity *philosophes*.

You must meet my dear aunt condition.
Quite a character, introductress
to mind's society. Conditions:

limit variety, put into categories, open reformatories
for the ill-conceived and misbegotten.
Accusatory crystallizers, reality's proselytizers,
keeping dossiers on active agents,
conditions can't fake it.

Now, no one "sees" conditions
by looking directly, by smelling and touching.

Conditions don't tingle the taste buds
or tickle your tenders.

One might catch a condition slant wise,
in glancing reflections; out of the corner
of one's eyes, or in the mist rising from a lake,
or in the state of being half awake.

Conditions are as clear as sky,
as fat as ducks, as loose as change.

About conditions it could be said:
there's scant relief to a puzzled head
when told it lies in conditioned beds.

Gnomenon

What is known by a gnome?
Stout perceivers of carrot root and anchor weight.
Do they wrangle categories, nudge notions
From some eschatologies of the depths?
Are gnomes known?

The perspicuity of a gnome's noggin
is not diluted by matter's wet mulch;
not glossed by a lipstick syllogistic,
not shrouded by a *"know not what"*.

Never lobotomized by numbing numerologies,
a gnome views (as it were) from below,
through illumination's indirect peep holes,
enchanting treasures of Truth, directly.

A gnome views Truth in three ways:
via composition – upended gold spill and hard sparkle;
via panpsychism – all know of that meant only for each;
via hypostasis – transfiguration of finder and found.

When gnomes nail a thing through thought
a matchbox village takes form
wherein are built (by rickety cause-ways)
subterranean city states.

In this way gnomes acquire
proper knowledge of their kind
and line their pockets with the wealth
of things unknown to mind.

Oracle Porch

Contemplating the difference
  of what is, and the identity
  of what is not, I take a bite

of sponge cake. The pores
  I spear with plastic forks
  that really hit the spot.

Now full, but not content,
  I'm thirsty. A negativity
  best remedied by tea.

So, taking a cup,
    saucer, and slice
      out to the porch
        I suck it up,

turning my attention
to the sneaky suspicions
of pure reason *as such*.

But sensing a certain limitation,
  I decide to think only
    of the actual,

of what appears, of what is natural.
  For what exists, in retrospect,
    like a humid, screened
      off porch in summer,
        deflecting pests,

is highly selective.
  This "I", like a glass
    of tea, is mystery.

But then comes malarkey, the fierce

dilemmas of survival, anarchy,
fighting with tooth and claw under

the laws of hierarchy, there's no
appeal, a down and dirty
dash to patriarchies

going *kersplat*
on the windshields
of history.

The absent sponge cake
mutters agreement, somewhere
in the pit of my gut. I think

that perhaps
it's not much
of a bad thing
to be sitting

in a screened off porch. In fact
it's time to drink a glass of port
and leave the logic to the cats.

Stir Fried

Her voice is even, her air
one of seasoned amusement.
               Messy,
but somehow quaint, "flavor,"
she explains, "holds strength."
A dash, perhaps,
              of bitters
into a pleasure-pan, stir fired.

The disciplined oil holds heat,
the aromatic blur of a spirit's
sigh. She claims this trick can-
not be taught, a tasty
              mix
of erudition. Or attitude? At best

the thawing of some snow peas seems
a given, or carrots diced together.
But her potions, treats, and hexes steam
             until it's all
                 crisp treasure.

Dinner With Duns Scotus

Cutting loose in a spectral palace,
a summa theologian heaps a plate
of steaming okra, ogling
the oddball units with a phantom's eye.

The oval kitchen puzzles him.
How to tell the difference
between one and many okra?
(In confirmation, the plates sparkle).

And he counts one, two, three.
Okra coats the platter's surface,
a metaphor of multiples,
an unnerving circus.

Because, okra lacks a plural, or
is it the singular no mind may know?
On knife's edge the obdurate tidbits roll.

For they have a modal color there,
he thinks. *Per accidens*?
With a diabolic fork he scrapes
the shapes into a tin.

Can one know them extra mentally
as formal or subjective?
Will our knowledge of reality
be forever proved defective?

But within the Mind of God

he believes that he can see
why onions are not okra,
and okra are not peas.

Meal Time Sonnet

To chase away the phantoms of regret,
We gather in the kitchen to prepare
A pot of grits, or omelets light as air,
Though tangy with a dash of vinaigrette.

How could one know the power of papaya
To calm the indigestion and the soul;
That parsley sprigs, and carrots in a bowl,
Could shame the finest veggies in Valhalla?

We spruce our fare with basil and cilantro,
That gives delight to every curious tongue.
We take the gifts of valley, mist, and sun,

And spread them on our buns, if one may say so.
And though at times the shades around us linger,
It never gets too late to sprinkle ginger.

At Times, Poetry

1.

Golden, fine
fur along the moon
of thigh,
her adorned ankles
are clouds shining.

Lizard candy,
a harness of jewelweed,
pomace and coriander
along a river of milk.

2.

Leaning against the cathedral door with the caprice
       of a jar lid,
chasing the flame of Orion and the smell of wet
       creek stone,
plaiting the loose hair of the vibrantly shaking souls
       of women,
braving the everlasting blue-green Diaspora of the
       maternal nest bed ...

3.

Then someone brings in a cactus.
Then the sun flows through a plastic cup.
Then God speaks in eleven separate cycles.
Then the angels brew my coffee.
Then a blue egret nuzzles my ear.
Then I am employed to tickle the bones of most women.
Then I am told to wash the feet of the beloved.

Then I am given something to spend wisely.

4.
A house.
A grave.
A Jesus tree.

5.
Mossy bloom of hemlock
at the bottom of a well,
the wall curving.

Her sensuous inclinations
are met with kindness.

What Are Poems?

Fruits of vapor and sediment,
pages, songs and thoughts, flags
unfurling in the wind, a curtain
of words, games of chance.

We are always piling rocks, one upon
the other. Hammering together with
bricks, fastening with bolts, sanding,
forming, fabricating, designing, planning.

An old poet in the woods over there,
his gray beard and patched clothing
varied like sunlight in the trees —
vodka laid him low. But then again
I saw him in those bright caverns
          of alcohol,
sat with him on tree stumps, whistling
tunes from the collective unconscious,
or floating proofs for the existence
of an "external world", or perhaps
          the presence
of another mind. I can tell you that this
cotton candy can rot your teeth out.
Best to keep a more substantial diet
than vodka and cotton candy.

Angelic apparitions slice the back
of my sleeping mind ... well, the blood
is comforting. And their perfections
          mock, in a way,
states that should just be accepted.

For example, these blueberries
are just what they should be. As were the gypsy-

31

moths who greeted me earlier. Poems
        can be like that.

A language of moods, perhaps. Songs
in defiance of time; paper glitter
and colored glass, a play of light
        on silver.

So what is included? Arrowheads
in bluegrass are preferable to orange peels
in dumpsters, but we will take the elements
as we find them. The soft yellow tongues
of buttercups might polish our thoughts,

and the roll of snake eyes might determine
our direction. The way the cards fall, or the ball
bounces, or lady luck smiles, or the posture
of a groundhog – all of these contribute.

And what are poems?

Are they a kind of rose? Clouds?

   They are always climbing,
climbing like snails mounting
        the parapets of
        temples,

   they are always closing,
closing like purple jonquils
        dotting the lush
        weeds,

they are always opening,
opening like chrysalides

in a bright
wind,

they are always falling
falling with the weight
of a thousand
flowers.

Lucky 13

Arias drift above your head in mother Mary clouds,
the color of your eyes like a new orange;
wherever you walk the flowers murmur among themselves,
your long legs tapping the earth in the key of C.
Small children and grown men, as well as a raccoon,
that had been living like a king in the parking lot dumpster,
threw themselves at your feet. You rose above them, O
you rose! Herbs, berries, a lemon and six slices of
watermelon
levitated toward your flowing locks but fell back,
heartbroken.
And your lips! Their pleasure was pure punishment;
luckily you took great pride in fulfillment
and your personal demeanor always unimpeachable –
you should have been president, but politics bored you.

We arrived at the oracle encountering more than one zenith
like a freight train bearing down on two martini sippers.
The old number 13, what a punch! We staggered about,
stumbled through weeds, tripped over a fossil, hit our heads
        on a fence …
the light just kept getting more and more bronze, everything
        was becoming a *riplet*,
then Diotima pushed us into the lake, where we performed
        exceptionally well, I thought …
so well in fact that Ms. D. compelled us to repeat ourselves
        several times over
and were thereafter awarded with a silver frosted tetragonal
        trisoctahedron,

which you promptly shellacked and placed in the livingroom.
Then scallops and anemones came alive in the skies over
        England
and you brought me a bowl of mint leaves and oxymorons,

34

whereupon I brushed my teeth and shined my face
hoping thereby to please you in ways provoking and
        delightful
suddenly my proud, isolationist self a courier of favors,
and you, in your splendid teleological ascendancy
more than a priestess, so rich in your eremite ways -
in one fell swoop inventing a new type of wine press
that we immediately christened with thirteen Latin surnames
(after which we were as drunk as balloons)
and we laid down to rest among the arias, the mother Mary
clouds our pillows and plain straw for a bed.

Fragments

1.

A tincture of snow, rose tipped,
the tiny tracks of a crow.
From off of the trees there slips
soft leaves in delicate rows.

2.

Her eyes are whispering stars.
Her words taper like the leaves
        of a white rose.
Her lips are speaking a language
        of moods.
While over her spine moves a shiver
like a trace of wind over water.

3.

On the grey street:
rummage of slicked gravel,
rotating lights in harlot chartreuse,
the scene outside, the dripping tin,
the eye narrowing in the wet frame.

In the dark bar:
vacancy at the table,
a sombrero and cardboard.
Ring the bell, its last call;
the cattle scatter
in the clover of afterhours.

4.

At last the sweet wine's purple breath
and the butterflies of April

have led me to those soft lit depths
where I become love's equal.
Falling my spirit soars, blue dreaming
a sharpened, starry light
that shines above the hills of evening
enclosed by night.

5.

Tool sheds, pot shards, bottle caps and buckets,
loose change, brass frames, candle wicks and sprockets,
wing tips, heart beats, whirl winded heirlooms,
dragonflies, fig trees, bookshelves and toadstools;
branching from the corridors of ocean, hill, and star light,
blue and silver moods quickly dress themselves in twilight.

6.

Awash in the autumn Appomatox, her optimal tinderbox
keen beaded like an Indian blanket,
exceeds in hot augur and lover's hysterium
the sinister alacrity of a spinster's aquarium.

7.

Aplomb of bright feathers, traveling moonlight,
owl eyes that wink to the elephant ears;
lemons of yellow, leaves of mint,
a spider spins; traps of honey drip.

Here at the river's break we scout for bone ringlets.
We scout the green lamps and the Indian blankets.
Beneath the white cloudfall, we travel the mist
that scouts the peachwood and the yellow thistle.

8.

Along the white sphere of the descending autumn moon

new stars hang from twilight curtains; the blue of cathedral
            glass
compels the return of long nights and deep dreaming.
Among dark hours a wandering current threads
the flowering stones.

9.

My cracked reflectors of light,
(modulations of mood)
edge clearly the lines on a leaf,
direct a flower's bearing,
are stained by fat spilling grapes,
hang loosely from the windows of churches.

And yet, behind us the glow of old suns
mock with pink impertinence
the somber of indolence.

10.

Moonshine parallelograms
stashed beneath medieval pews
invigorate my typed verbatims.

Where perennial boutonnieres
pinned to blue collars
are quite spherical;
their vertebrae tacked
to endless cultivation.

11.

A patch of starry violets,
the crystal chime of mandolins;
beneath the soft coin of her navel
a sudden euphony

like gold threads in a cloud.

And beyond all mourning
she is tossed on the silver
of thickets and bird song
that hold the sky's root.

12.
Dropping blackberries into stone cups
Where the diamonds blush like roses.

13.
The prismatic shine of an hourglass
shall track the swirl of fire into blue,
where totems fly their space, and clouds
that roll and break will lift the inside out.

14.
From out of the crushed
palm and the rusted nail
rose petals drift
on a summer wind.

Blind Spot

Light scattering in shallow water:
the gold rim of oblivion, soul's window
caked in tones of silver and rust.

Archaic tintypes of longing.
A parrot drifting the blues.
The old bird rattles *"esse est percipi"*

which lacks something
when I remember her voice:
the percipient won't hold your hand.

Leaved figures in green.
The young entwine themselves,
are branching, conspiring,
pearling around their tables
like drops on a glass, in summer.

One could be born again
or reworked and born bitter
without progress. *Percipi.*

The sun waxing.
Talking like lovers talk.
I had grown older.

They were holding hands and smiling

Stairwells

Looking down, the steps always appear to wind clock-wise,
following the slope of density, a kind of reticulated
falling; perhaps an exit sign or a locked door, surveillance
cameras, aura of the inorganic enclosures that secure us

from ourselves. What goes up must come down. But the
vice-versa need not apply. The peculiar effect of ascension
(a suppression of awareness?) *is* the tilting lope of vertigo ...
procession and decline ... gravity's playhouse,

a pop-up book among cigarette butts, suddenly,
"you have to take the stairs", there is something
out of whack, time to climb, as floors slip by
you look down to see it, a mine shaft, an invitation

to free fall, but each step is a place, identical,
leading to the next, as you fall asleep, the letter
falls open, the pit, the abyss, the sudden realization
of leaves falling, as we change, we take the stairs

to go up, for we have been down. The stairwell
is the spine of the spatial beast, otherwise
top and bottom collapse. Place loses definition,
leaves have no corner to gather, there is no sweeping,

everything lies flat on the plain. The great American mid-
west, so flat, the heart land, perfect for highways,
the endless fields of asphalt, how sad to be deprived
of slopes, precipice, canyon, to have a sky that cannot

be approached. No tower of Babel,
no echolocation, we erect
our multi-storied idols, spires that define a city
like quills on a porcupine's back, no country lassitude

41

here, nothing laid back in this megaplex of double dealers,
they take the stairs. It is a healthy cardiovascular
tuner upper. They take them to the top of the stocks;
to the bottom of retail. The journey (they say) is why
we have them, the lonely stairwells, the passageway.

Ocarina

The native slipstream of his breath
adjusts an octave on the ocarina. An
open calyx of a reed, a sound that slips,
tips, and trips between stamens, stones,
seeds. The texture iridescent, the presence
of a wind-tone. So personal, a delicate

hand carved instrument tapping the temples
of his sensibility. So many tunes! So much
restless wind stirring the sea's salty floor:
soul, the egg, emblem of his wishes;
the ocarina sings beneath the pressure
of his perennial noodling. With the persistence

of a hunting javelina, he plays in creeks,
bluffs, nooks and crannies; the soft blow
repentant, applying a rough and ready prayer
to the trestles of his surroundings. On one knee
he recalls a glint of tourmaline, amethyst,
steep pinnacles in occasional mist, high

cotton. He gives thanks for the opacity
that redirects rather than reflects
the gusts and gales of his intended rhythms
(more intense now, the inward current
that lavishes a play upon the ocarina).
Opaled in a pleasant mix of visions

he's game for a theophany, part of nature's
concertina. A scratch that needs an itching,

this soft teasing, this Sapphic sophistry
is polished on his sleeve; a sofa troubadour,
he learns to breathe, to initiate the weather,
to preen the nights, to keep a constant measure.

Houses And Trees

Footstool to squirrels, and pigeon heavy rookery
        a house of wood,
          needing paint
and sitting ponderously among pecan trees, oak, and ash

where a slightly evaporative attic sheds its trash
        from leaf stuck gutters
        apparently on the lean,
over a driveway of gravel, pebbles, shells, concrete:

among asphodel and mistletoe, the infrastructure quaint
        in a morning perched
        at thoughtful angles,
unlike the blind and cramped tangles of subdivided slums

where the bottom line has turned the elegant dumb.
        Houses that were once
        trees that breathed
the blue into a legendary sky, now lie like lazy bums

in huddles, antibiotic products for watching cable,
        microwaved treats
        (or tasteless traces)
sliced into the thinnest available spaces. It seems to be

that the older ones were bolder, places with history, nobler
        in trills, a certain beauty
        breathing intricacy,
spare, a respect for the privacy of what's bare, a stair-

well sleek, or a stained glass door. Oracles for tourists,
        some. But others

       in scattered lots,
in dishabille, exist in limbo, rot. That burned out giant,

there, now overrun with vermin, once rented space
       to a famous frat. In fact
       the liquor swilling brats
in a hazy, beer stained rush set the poor house ablaze,

or another, not far away, played host to women's clubs
       in 1929. Now it fades
       almost murmuring, imaginary,
like the supernumerary mutterings of a ruined monastery,

or the abandoned rooms of a YMCA. But the trees
       giving leaves and shade
       declare that what is grown
is hermitage to life, God's scaffold for whatever roams.

Beside A Pool

Some say I spent my youth on bathtub gin.
I never learned to swim, but truth be told:
I'd gladly trade my thumbs for supple fins.

Some say I am too dumb to save my skin.
Some say with work I'm quick to fold.
Some say I spent my youth on bathtub gin.

To coral castles set in marshy dens
A current takes me on a gentle roll;
I'd gladly trade my thumbs for supple fins.

On sparkling waves my senses start to spin.
The flowers dry my feet and make be bold.
Some say I spent my youth on bathtub gin.

I see a school of fish and envy them,
But elders at their labors leave me cold.
I'd gladly trade my thumbs for supple fins.

I pray to God I never get the bends!
But then again I'd rather not grow old ...
Some say I spent my youth on bathtub gin.
I'd gladly trade my thumbs for supple fins.

In The Sticks

Beyond poles of cacti and buttermilk light
there are grasslands and rock bottoms deep,
where green crocodiles gather to greet,
exchange wives, and sharpen their bite,

where the umbilical chords
of their cries, red arroyos
and sand storming skies,
belabor a theory of mine
on the break water leverage of time.

Where the crocks
in emerald skins and eyes that are drowsily coy
lay snares,
while snouts breaking out of round edible shells
sniff air.

There tick against tock turns long,
antique clocks chime meandering songs
of jigsaw puzzles at noon,
of spiders at play in our brooms.

Under The Influence

Those girls are stoned, their silly words
disturb the surface of the air, slim winged
mosquitoes rising on this summer's day.
Around my lily pads they buzz; the ground
is moist, the granite pools reflect
a terra cotta angel's tragic smile.

Here hidden speakers leak unending noise,
and drinks are pink as roses, ivy laced,
wet, sagging like the kisses of a cloud.
I skitter, a lizard with an agile tongue
that darts between the girl's bare feet.
Those girls are stoned, they face

a string of Christmas lights (now strung
like ne'er do wells around the corners of a tree)
that hasn't worked in years. The birds
toss them away, the squirrels brush them aside,
while from a very privileged point of view
I sweep the dreaming, antique steps

of luscious moans from out of limestone cracks,
from out between the stoned girl's pretty toes,
translucent shards as bright as broken glass.
A damn good thing, because the labyrinth
can always use a touch up, now and then.
Stoned girls ... perhaps they could be held

to blame for cloudy skies that alternate
between unknown and undetermined colors.

There is no way to tell, form where I sit,
forever locked outside the gates of better moods,
on rusted lawn chairs, condensing into salty drops
that wet the rising goose bumps on their skin.

Automotive

Top light under the engine coils,
red loop oscillating,
hot acid heads, bitter tips,
and a fine resistance of green.
Cracks beneath the suspicious eye,
then a clean break, an answer.

Possibility can tangle unpredictably,
can tango across the searching mind.
Seeing the police lights, the fear in retrospect,
usually *not* in the ratchet force, not
in the light switched on, then off.

Decimal signature turns the weather,
purveyor of ornaments, hood, and dash:
from the rear view mirror, under the compartment
we are signaled and sent packing, pieces of trim.

Shale and stucco, don't test me,
don't toss me onto the gravel of shoulders
where vacant houses spill into tree lines
and a mine shaft gone bust.

Turn us toward the shoreline.
Stroke the caliper, shine us in chrome and copper.
Kick us in rows of vibrant heat,
gliding above sparks and wrecks
that sing in this dripping storm of wheels.

Gardener's Tale

Out back among the smooth cut stumps
of trees gone to heaven, I turn a spigot
to rinse my tools (spade, rake). The sun

is kind today. I trudge, a caravan of one,
among varieties of color: crispheads and leeks
red turnips, orange melons. Here are rampions

and mandrakes, there is seed and plot rotation.
The sodden mulch is rich, and in my eyes lovely.
I tend to rows that germinate, scraping a ration,

pruning and trimming. This is a gift, turning time
into an appetizer. Here on the soon to be salads
of a working garden, I lay a sprinkler's trace

onto shoots and climbers. Although best raw,
and whether culinary or medicinal, the nodding
blooms of an apothecary, of amaranthus, of china

berry, settles my thoughts into the comfort
of their moist beds. My mind occupies
the yard, becoming loose leafed, considering

chards, fuzzing over as if in love, or at least
hungry for a decent lunch. A pinch of cloves,
or carrots in a bunch, I am careful among

the cauliflower, my respect extends to those
who keep it clean: spiders, a praying mantis,
spotted mantids on the wing. I touch a snap-

bean among pods of Christmas peppers; I lean,
intangible as a mustard seed, tending to paprika,

striking my spade into the earth, seeding fields,

wiping my face with a cabbage leaf. It seems
a kind of resurrection made real. Root savior
of the compost, my mixtures do the trick,

utilizing the efficacy of waste, the true worth
of things gone to pasture: rusted fixtures, a shed,
the left over alchemy bled from old containers,

a life concentrated into cultivated space,
in love with this work, with the dirt, with sweat,
with the shovel and fret of a garden's grace.

Archaic Memory

Then the sky darkened, full of wind and vengeance,
shot through with lightning and drenching squalls,
moving across the earth like a nameless army
        bent on slaughter.

In a reed basket we were sent drifting
to the banks of the red river, the black sky
arching above us like a funeral pyre, burning
        through nightfall.

We reached shore, taking the form of siblings,
building a habitation of weeds and mist,
roaming along the marshy banks in anger,
        where we subsisted

on the tender flesh of cactus leaves,
on the smooth surface of the curving purple
plums that nestle in a bed of summer,
        sweetened and falling;

and in the morning, when the clouds subsided,
when oranges were cut and jelly dappled,
when eggs were whipped, when the sun had warmed
        a kitchen window,

you were lying propped among pillows,
rubbing the warmth into your legs, and smiling,
your hair disheveled, your eyelashes sweetly
        whispering sleep;

your skin smooth as cotton, and giving,
our bodies resting and moving at leisure,

following the secret orbits of the divine
        sphere luminous.

Awaken to me only, my love.
For we are abandoned, left to wander,
left to sort these porous grains
        of rose seed.

Appear in earthly form, lost ally,
and we will read the paper, or chew on ice cubes
or talk metaphysics, or fan each other
        with elephant leaves.

Place your shield at the door of remorse.
Shower, by the light of lemons and snowflakes,
our thoughts with the colors of divinity,
        dear heavenly muse.

Solar

The uncoiling winter sun
shatters
into golden drops,
melting on the tongues of Pan.

The milkweed's sharp
precipitate
weans the budding lamps
that float on northern winds.

There the lakes are cold
and victorious.
There the blue unmoving surface
brocades the stars of heaven.

There Sappho composes
in shapes appearing
crescent, white ethereal,
a morning frost
over the cherry trees.

And there, she blossoms
in jeweled eclipses,
shining
with aerial wings,
with the gold
of broken bracelets.

Evening's Shadow

Signals

We are building a fire up in the hills,
gathering marshmallows, garlic cloves,
braids of trellising flowers, beer cans,
radishes, gourds for jack o' lanterns;
all high above the edges of expressways,
      the sidewalks
of neighborhoods, higher than the tilt-
yards of churches, above the paths
      of easy climbing.

Often when roaming these rocky slopes
among quail and spotted deer, foxes,
scorpions and tarantulas, it becomes clear
that a game of chance is in play.
      The numbers
are impersonal, although it is fun to pretend
that they plot for us. There is an alchemy
at work, a transmigration of material.

Once these hills were mined for silver.
Even before the internal combustion
engine, they wandered on mule backs,

picking at the dry earth. There is no more
silver now, that lonely substance. Only
the moon, which does not grieve
      or number past regrets.

As seems to happen
where human habitation once thrived

but now lies abandoned
the harvest of night has grown lush:
the owls have come back, as well as phantoms,
violets, wild grapes, a lost rosary, a mirage.

The land is owned by the government.
There are no masses on these abandoned
hill sides. Instead, someone has built
a deep-dish-radio-space antennae. Paper
money, now freed from its mineral chains,

was spent by the billions for this miracle
of metal. One cannot see the signals
charging up both girder and pinion
to be cast forever into endless space.

There has at yet been no reply.

How many times can one be slapped away
          from the table
and still maintain an ardor for perfection?

We have built our fire behind it. A cold
night, bright with flashing stars, illumines
a stark edifice. The station, like a casino
          seems to float
          in darkness.

Outside of the fire's peripheral glow
a desert opens. The wind sweeps down,

moving the silent figure. Judas hanging
          from a tree limb,
Christ delivered into the hands
          of his enemies.
They are laying the body down, and moving on.

Disciples, being unoriginal, are in despair.
The ornamentation of his words
has become a kind of death in life,
and a life in death. High above them,
from some distant and unimagined world

the station's signals, a kind of celestial
light, falls without favor upon the gilded
archways, upon the open mesa, upon the
          star drunk gardens.

While above our fire, a blue nimbus
holds the moon in a feathering aura,
reflecting the light of our desires
in departing tones of silver.

Collectibles

Scattered, in need of recollection
on the banks of the forked river,
pursuing the found luminous,
the moods made visible:

Lynx Eye:
Prismatic shield of light, your spectral allure
entwining aggregates of color; sensitive
to the pressure of spectrums, open this gate
to the center stage, display and raise
       your blue curtain.

Fool's Gold:
A brittle spark in distortion's light
false sharpened, with lies enameled,
thin lipped, your deposits cheat
       the desperate seeker.

Obsidian:
Collapsing center of light, whirlpool
of demonic attraction, desire's end
glowing against your unseen backdrops,
       in darkness brooding ...
travel the outline of the unspoken
       covering under.

Pyrope:
From the sparks of the turning earth
flaring rose red and blood petaled,
out of the parabolic chamber a flame,

a burning coal.

Coral:
Among the soul's host, in the richness
of creation, rolled in the palm of time,
attraction of elements. Bloom in deep
remembrance, collecting and emerging.

Backyard

part of the acre
holding the kindling
for our bonfire
was overgrown with sassafras
and prickly pear;

a jejune
bramble of feelers
in a land not unlike
Lilliput, not
attractive real estate.
pin pricks

from the thick
pyracantha, dead
vines and fire
ants forming
tricky steps to an ash bed
of sparks, finger

fed, blazing upward
into the aura
of the backyard dark;
our drunken eyes
dilated, stinking of
whiskey sours,

we jumped through
the licking flame,
catching air, wild

in our tiny wilderness,
filled with oomph,
landing on our boots.

Wooden Nickels

Living in the servant quarters
of sweat and desperation
where desires are soup bones
in the witch's kitchen,

the curvature of space
and the soft brush of patterns
cover the floor boards
like sawdust petals.

Do not confuse the meaning
with coquettish symbols.
Do not conflate the physical
with the signs of things spiritual ...
Says the leaf blown sun
bathing in a prolegomenon of light.

What looks nicer behind glass
where also a sundial illuminates
eleven different shades of rust?

The old testaments
of stamina and color.

A Day In The Country

Crocodile sleeping
Yellow sharpened leaves
Crawdads on a string
Leather tied to bark

Shotgun in the weeds
Pigeons in the cane
Sugar, pepper, twine
Oven, chimney dust

Twining, buttons sewn
Old are speaking new
Do they "search for love"
Searching "for someone"

Church is full of bloom
Land is thick with lust
Christ returns a groom
Trucks interred in rust.

Long Division

Leaf and cloud arranged, a subtle equation,
formulae of whispering chimeras, the troubled air …
among the trees the sense of a deep geometry
embracing.

Embracing the equidistant ratio of grapes.
Embracing the curve of starlight, the wine glass
ellipsis, the perpendicular flash of surface
and stem.

An atmosphere coordinate, ephemeral,
transparent …
leaving secretly coded remnants
on a red map book.

Evening Song

As day completes
Its tired and necessary arc

Pale clouds of ice
Sail through the deepening sky.

The wine is dark and red.
The stars shine in it.

Tilted to her lips
They are rising and disappearing.

When the Hunter's moon rises
To the eye of the mind
Her heart's aim takes shape
Sweeping through the land like dreams.

More Wine

Round red, my droplets
of spilt wine collect, deep
rubies in the twilight.

Outside the showers came
and went, as the carpet
lay breathing. I was thinking

that in old skins it's so hard
to start sometimes,
while the smell of cut weeds
and mating cats drift through
my doorway.

By the window a silver emblem
turns in the wind, metallic corkscrew,
slide lightning on its dark surface.

And what I want confronts me,
forcing me slant-wise into the wet
ivy. Well, that's where I sit,

watching the snails glide
along the edges of an evening rain.
Somewhere the night pond, whispering,
divides beneath uncertain hands.

The Uncovering

Behind new masks the self can hide
And dance beyond the falling leaf.
I looked within and found the self outside.

Moving like music, shapes spark and slide
Bundled into a lonely sheaf.
Behind those masks the self can hide.

Where comes the silver hues that light a dream,
Or scents that rise when roses cleave the air?
Looking within, I see the self outside.

For when the frame, draped in light, appears
And whether weaved with feather, scale, or hair
Behind bright masks the self can hide.

Within each mind there shines a mirrored gleam,
A glass through which we read a message there:
To look within, and find the self outside.

The falling starlight clothes us like a bride.
We sigh among the orchids and the trees.
Behind this mask the self could hide,
I looked within and found the self outside.

Widower

Empty, this house, and vacant
This lapis lazuli, changing
Memories, elegies, regrets,

A spectral kingdom wandering,
Revolving and turning towards
         hidden sources;

Eliciting the unmanifest,
Every color epigamic, a sound
Like the high cirrus of evenings,

The air chill, the cinquefoil
Of petals in the mind's cavatina
         opening inward:

Like a lonely satellite spinning
Under the feet of the Naiads,
By the trunk of the Tamarind,

Beetles, buttons, roots and stems
Of strawberries and tulips bending
         wet with rain:

Nectarines on a copper plate,
Among millipedes, a pearl
In a nest of paper and string;

Something torn, a book, pages
Of empty icons, there is no one
         home.

Dark Shines A World

Dark shines a world
where the passing is all
        that is seen,
where over the ruins entwine
        laurels of green.

Where the sky
like the shape of the moon
        in a flowering river
        flows white,
and the kisses of lovers burn
        jewel-like
        in opulent night.

Where the mind
is caught by a dream of impossible forms
        not found,
and the souls of the world rotate in mysterious
        sound.

On the graves,
pale roses in bloom draw the light
of the evening star down,
and the shadows of wings
        pass silently
        over the ground.

Dark shines a world
where the sweat of the passionate face
is cooled by patterns of lace,

windy sunlight and infinite space.

Try A Locked Door

At different times the promise of illusions come
To tease the burdened mind
And color with intensity the laboring breath
That rises, like the surface of a wall
Enclosed
By points of empty space;

Where stairwells of ascending and descending steps
Coil, bordered by an iron arm
That wanders to the double sided doors of halls
Where indecision and regrets
Revolve.
Try a locked door.

Because we do not know the force a turning brings
Except that here is what we have become
And feel the weight of every moment passing through
Like repetitions of an act of shame:
Again,
No lifting of the wind.

What's hard to say is harder yet to live.
In memory the vacant rooms cry loud.
If then our fragile understanding fails
And what defines us comes to be
Our jail,
Try a locked door.

Everything That Burns

Everything that burns is trash:
all the promising games that welcome
a player, all the lonely nights,
the lottery tickets, the personal ads,
all the schools, anybody with a bit
of advice, those that smile and mean
nothing, those that smile and hide
everything; flying insects, canned goods,
unwashed dishes; emotions wrenched,
disabled, and discarded.

Anything can burn,
and everything that burns is trash.

However, there are truths beyond doubt.
For example: I am a fool (therefore etcetera).

The ravages of fire.
My hands are swollen now,
my lips have lost all, even
the worst expectations ...
and when my mouth fell vacant
I knew I had lost you.

Set me up.
I am trash that burns.

Everything that burns is trash:
fire heals with time the destroyer,
destroying and leveling with time,

with all of the mercy of gravity,
with all of the power of atoms
splitting in a void.

No pity.
The pity of the empty field.
The pity of the open waste.

Everything that burns is trash:
the stars, the banks, the homes,
the bars,
the jobs, the trees, this mind.

And yet ...
you are standing in the distance
like a diamond
forged by the fiery pressure
of my desire.

But you are only an image
and ideal, and so beyond all fire.
My love, this fire cannot touch you.

And as the fire burns slowly down
a mirror shines silver and cold.

It stands alone.
Everything that burns is trash.

Requiem

The curls of her hair are white like the moon,
The blue in her eyes as cold as a stone,
The fruit of her orchard more bitter than blood,
So pray for the ones who are buried by love.

The words of the heart are mirrored in glass,
The vows of desire escape with the wind.
The sins of our passion drain out with our blood,
So pray for the ones who are buried by love.

So pray for the ones who are buried by love
And sing for swift passage from out of the grave:
The fruit of her orchard more bitter than blood,
The stain of her lips is the closing of day.

So sing for swift passage from out of the grave.
The sins of our passion drain out with our blood.
The blue in her eyes as cold as a stone,
The curls of her hair are white like the moon.

The vows of desire escape with the wind.
So pray for the ones who are buried by love.

Outline

A. <u>Introduction</u>:
1.) *Time* is the curve of a woman's thigh,
true and impartial and beyond explanation.
2.) *Feeling* is the unfolding flower, soft awakening
of teardrop and cloud fall.
3.) *Hope* comes later, a distillation of the vision
temporalized
(it is the dew itself, soft as tears, a residue of surfaces).

B. <u>Argument</u>:
1.) Here one might insist upon the lie of privacy,
or opt for the false social:
2.) Fidelity or free love, two horns of a devil
3.) That roots without planting or sows without
knowing.

C. <u>Conclusion</u>:
1.) Graves mark the surface as feelings turn to tears,
and back again.
2.) Tears reflect the morning dew, turning to clouds.
3.) Behind the marker hope lies drunk and slumbering,
waiting.

Pea Coat

A pea coat
of double breasted wool, classic sailor's
wrap against the salty swell of winds,
covered him like an army tent amid
his wandering life – homeless, jobless,
reading philosophy and doing weird
narcotics, standing on corners, his judgment

unraveling slightly
as he peered into the windows of untended
homes, alone among the mating cats,
his vision panchromatic, varying between
states of the dissolute and the ecstatic,
his hair a matted hat, his teeth
in tatters, a cold notion like a remnant

draped his shoulders
as snug as any shawl, a turtle on the crawl
that hefts its house upon its back, he stared
in a kind of telemetrical terror at
what he had become, awash like fallen plums,
no chance for self-respect, his prospects lost,
his old rank kicked to smithereens

like a lunch box
dismantled on the playground of his past.
Fate, an old maid principal with a prying eye,
with a whistling board whipped his bare behind.
If only the ferocious forms that populate his head
could dictate a goal, he might succeed. And yet
inside, he finds no genius, but a bowl

full of dumb ideas

79

perpetuating the remedial tendencies
of his bones. Like the sticking point of whatever
could be known, his memories, curtain to a reality
as wooly as a pea coat, serve as epaulets upon
his Orphic attire, cushioning his groans, like diplomas
from the school of fire, or spray upon the sea.

Madness Stirs

At every point the slow slush skids,
one turns around, goes down, down
to the bottom rungs, to sanity's salty edge,
sits on the very ground, against a wall.
No family there, no friends. But look,
something slithers, something forks

a tongue into the dark –
an iguana prowls in sassy folds of skin
with blue around the eye,
glistening green and pearlish in the murk.
It is company of sorts
and it points with its snout to a route

that rises, as if through burning shame,
in brisk flame toward a raised bridge.
Walk down it then, it's easy to fall off
and be buried like some dirty treasure
in the loam. The spasms come at night
when madness stirs. Alone

at dawn is worst, because
there's nothing but the dull hung over head
to greet the sun. All day
to plod from one place to the next,
scorched nerves that scrape
or strike like snakes, like iridescent

birds. This is mechanical venom,
crazy lies, where diamonds decompose

and echoes multiply. To be named
is what it hates, for under focus
it cannot fecundate, while seraphs
strategize a stalemate to its game.

Moving

When they knocked the last block down
to chalk and rubble, paved the river bank,
left him to wander among the steel girded
skeletons rising from the flattened ground

it was time for moving. High rent had washed
his savings down the drain, and so, on a lame
and dingy bus, with the spoils of one pay day
and a half-assed plan and a piece of weather

vane (kept as a souvenir from the old house),
he headed out, down the nautical 20/20 of interstate
everywhere. Sleepless, one of the modern nomads,
uprooted, afloat above asphalt, shot like a pinball

down the throats of America on the sprawl,
the infrastructure rusty, coughing up the musky
hydrocarbons doing their work on the atmosphere,
no nearer where he should be than at anytime

in any other lair, subject to rolling black outs
and the bare necessities provided by a Quicky
Market's pilfered wares, he picked a tenement
and settled there. Then stuck around

and called the damn thing *square*.

Please Explain

Where have you been, sparkle?
Where have you gone, candle?
Will we imbibe no more of Tertullian's
       high lingo?

I shrink from the freezing dark
of interstellar space. I cannot
even keep my bookshelves free
       of this dust,

much less all that. And I'm allergic
to the remnants of worlds crushed
by collapsing supernovas (moons
       tickle my nose).

Whirling galaxies ... to "where" do they go?
Not to my room I can tell you.
I need more perspective ... more back bone

to accept finalities with equanimity.
I've begun collecting erasers
to prep for the Big Rearrangement.

Where did you say you were? The expanse of terra firma
like an apple straight from the mouth of *Deus sive Natura*
whetted my appetite for rose petals and brandy.
I thirst under this starry, brittle sky.
Come back, good feeling. Come back.

The Nominalist

Presented with the olfactory residue
of a carpenter's smooth work bench,
he declared it nugatory. No hoary
skein of universals for him,
no lurid stain of unanalyzable events:

the world as it truly is, *in reality*,
was bare as bones, or in a nifty
nutshell: thou shalt not multiply
entities beyond necessity.

No *quid rei.*
The color of moods?
Mere names. Any essence
brought shame. He stood now,
the bulletin in hand, his glands
perspiring, his sweat cooling
the heated thrashing given to illusions

in the figurative vein. Having finally rooted
the scoundrel from his lair, he mounted
the stone steps to his church office. Doctor
Invincibilis – the title gave him pleasure,
the name *venerabilis inceptor* considered

hard won treasure (although,
according to his philosophy,
titles meant nothing, apparently).
He remained, in the truest sense,
rebel without a cause, without even the trinity,
or the notion of effect, or immanent divinity,
or a platonic realm of law.

One could not know by reason,
but by faith. Overturned, upended,
cut into a worm fed mix of orphaned terms,
the grand project of synthesis fell baked.

No lucidity in the supra-totality, but a (w)hole
opaque, and, for the barber,
this was not just any face. *Being*
had been shaved. What had Ockham wrought?

A razor that had sliced away our high
day dreams, leaving concrete beams, a vacant loft,
an empty realm divided with no way to cross?

Interludes

Distinguish cactus leaves.
Do names have things?
Someone had said so.
Tomorrow the border?

Broken glass, cold star,
silver napkins on the bar.
Had a wife in Pedernales
federales called her Alice.

The station is white adobe.
Is that a passport?
Too early in the day
to think such a thing.

Policia! Policia!
Demon in my soul's tequila.
Caballero, two sombreros,
fatter than an angel's arrow.

A rusting epilogue.
Where's Lavaca?
Ten penny shoes;
brimstone.

Little bauble on a string
go to church to be a thing.
Even so, you're not filled up.
Have another whiskey cup.

Lazaretto

On the soundless drift of emptiness
he offered his hand, a sick thing:
deceased, depopulated
of the quicksilver attributes that kindle desire.

His face in pantomime, a funereal mask.
Repulsed by his presence in open daylight,
the underbelly of his dreams
floats to the world's surface, almost touching.

He has swept the broken crown away.
Relieved of the scepter, he is ready:
the white leaf opening;
his flight, his curve in the atmosphere of chance.

And although entombed by willful sightlessness,
their disgust and spite releases him,
an avatar unfolding,
dismantling every mirror in the archway of remorse.

And as he moves forward, the stone rolls away,
with shafts of light piercing, dust rising,
legs stepping, arms trembling:
"their terror against me, my longing, my reaching ..."

Harvester

From the grain house
where the lapidary teapot and the iron skillet
tempts the farm mouse,

buttered bread, sweet corn, and a celery spread
entices the ghost
to harness itself on a row of glass plates,

while the kettle brings soup to a simmering heat,
red oil and vegetable skin
incarnates this scaffold with color and flesh.

On the silo
where the light sheaves long amid nettles of dust
past the known lane

and falls in an arrow of showering rust
tapping each bone
with finalization of thumb and forefinger,

we partake on a table of green weave and tears
as the turning earth
gives amorous taste to a vision's hard touch.

Season's End

The hedge gone to straw, each winter tree disrobed,
the sloughing bark falling in broken chips,
a disentangling of summer's costume, the dry brush
sends the dove flying through trails of ice and cloud.

The lake is blue and silent and cold.
Tree stumps emerge like fingers from a glove.
Upon their sharp tips a hawk leans poised,
his avian sight skirting for a tell-tale sign.

He soars: as crawdads crawl and minnows mark time.
Ascending, his eyes skimming, he sees the colors
below him, gliding and turning;
his reflection on the lake

turns when he turns, glides when he glides
as if tied by hidden strings:
invisible relation, one moving to the other

as the hawk, finding its prey,
descends to attack
in a sudden flash,
plumes in the wake of the water's fine spray.

Principles

I.

Say hello to the outback. Find a trail
or fashion one with any tool at hand.
We have only uncertain directions,
          not much daylight,
          there are some clouds,
          we will need to get on.
Prowl carefully with an eye toward the rare
stone, or the silent wildflower opening
to the leisurely embrace of twilight.

Exhibits of old Polaroids, faded colors,
patterns dripping, a continual erosion,
a breaking off of pieces, edges smoothing,
meteorites roaming, shellfish floating,
tectonic plates slipping. The traffic of being

shuttles to and fro. Often, while passing along
this landscape, I have felt like some jack o' lantern
haphazardly carved. And yet, despite the bricolage,
my suspicion is that Principles litter these grounds
          like Easter eggs.
          But how to find one …
Attention to detail, perhaps. But luck seems
so much more desirable. Some call it grace,
some fortune. Principles? I would just like
          to hold one
in my hands, and turn it in the sunlight.

I keep imagining what they are made of.

Something reflective? Like tourmalines
or mercury? Something dense - like gravity

or dark moods? It seems that the only available
material is forever drifting, forever changing,
like sandstone or cardboard.

The spare attractiveness of a tree budding
in early spring. That could be one. Also
the plushy cushion of three leaf clovers. Also
the order of color at the close of day ... No.

Something's missing. These are just fuzzy
images, good for kissing, perhaps, or rubbing
during periods of stress. The puzzle won't
fill out. What is lacking? Rectitude? A sense
of the enduring? An idea of permanence?

Did the fossilized life forms caught in sediments,
the petrified wood, the mineralized deposits
of our ancestral noggin' scratchers, did they
engage themselves in questions of fortune,
          of grace?

I seem to recall pondering the internal arrangements
and the external arrangements – tossing bone joints,
          or reading the soggy entrails
          of a goat.

Certainly they tried their hands

at framing the big picture,
investing their portion of energy
 into the symbolic system.

Toss a pebble into the water. The impact
ripples like a sudden emotion. We can tremble
just on the edge of it, suspending breath,
delaying arrival, silvery tremors vibrating
like wet electrical wires, like musical strings.

The trick is not to fall off, to continue
          our balancing act
until the picture comes into focus.

          II.
Planted in sundial arcades, the white crosses
are relaxing. The violent deaths they represent
are covered over with St. Augustine grass,
                    platitudes.

A sprinkler system keeps the whole field
irrigated. Often the continuous and inescapable
misapplication of our time takes on a sinister shade.
Personal responsibility. Personal responsibility.

Yes, yes. I must remember
that I'm to blame for how it all turned out.
The problem, I think, is my pillow. It is not
          one of downy fleece,
          not golden swan,

not silver minx,
not ostrich down.
My pillow is stuffed with the infinite regress,
an unusual animal, and one that does not
provide a very sound night's sleep.

It is rumored
that there exists an antidote to the infinite regress.
They call them foundations. But the recipes
I've seen appear contrived, the solutions spurious.
Always it is the worst of us who are pushing them.

What gives fuel to suspicions of a general kind?
A table supports a certain
effort just now, and a chair, paper, etcetera.
Embodiment implies dependence
of every conceivable type. But the soul –
its job could almost be defined as a sort

of free fall, an endless drifting from something
to something else. But – the "seat" of the soul?

Something is leaving the city. The bus
moves through the humid night,
roaring like the mouth of Hades.
        Sit calmly.

The headlights are streaking from front
to back. Angry spirits. Someone is cursing,
someone crying. A baby lies with its hands

against the mother.

Beneath the aquamarine glow of the interior
the hand that cuts the deck can almost
be seen. A pair of nines, a king, a queen.
The aces seem far away, and elusive.
A deuce threatens to wreck the unsuspecting.

The dealing itself is mechanical, sightless,
the players accepting their fates
        without expression.

In the middle of nowhere the bus comes to a stop.
The ground below them is uneven and treacherous.
They must find a foothold, a purchase,
something stable, a foundation, or risk falling
        into absolute darkness.

Round

A silver heraldry of clouds
intones the advent of a mood,
the touch of distant melody

drifting in the fall of storms,
descending with the sudden rain,
rising on the cries of love.

Upon the open flowers
green and lavender pools
fill the tender cups and overspill.
The swell is in the leaves,
the grass, the trees; the lakes are filled;
the circular flowing, the overflow of life.

A cold sweeping wind
carries the solitary drops.
Here and there,
fine rays of sun
fall through a turbulent grey.

Creating, here and there,
warm circles of light,
gold coins laying in a field.

You are in these places.
I see you in a pearl of water.
I see you in the sun's bright reflection.

Limeade

I.

Gone, gone. Sad years.
You held such promise, once.
But perhaps all dreams are false.

What happened to you?
Everyone that you knew
Thought that you were the zip-ah-dee-doo,
And that everything that you said
Was true.

Slipped on a lime. Broke my shoe.

II.

But wait. Who is it that ... that truly knew you?
In the distance lies the very face of mystery.
Now she is presenting to me
A basket of green limes.

III.

Strange. That limes have their own "light".
For no one says: he has had his day
In the lemon light.

I may not doubt that two limes
And two limes make four limes.
I may not doubt that alone which

97

Experiences the lime.

IV.

For truly I say unto you:
That I will no longer flame out
In undulating spangles of lime.

For truly I say unto you:
That anyone who grows a lime tree
Shall sparkle.

V.

Some of the limes are tacky,
Some of the limes are smooth.
Some of the limes are wacky,
While some go well with Vermouth.

VI.

Who is it that has come in here
With the gift of limes?
A young woman speaks
With words that are silent.

Her very thought is luxury.
Quaestiones quodlibetales?
The lime has no distinctions.

VII.

Voices from the back patio
And the cool afternoon air.
How thrilling it was!

The young boy squeezes
With his hand his bright
        Lime.

VIII.

Are there no lime trees in this town?
Not anymore.
There is only the dark
And what comes after the dark.

IX.
        .

For all things will be made new.
And all will be well, and all will
Be made one, and all manner
Of things will be as one

In the limelight.

Carousels

Daybreak. The cabin leans a bit,
is set far back beneath a tangle of poplars.
The sound of the woods echoing;
       falling stars,
       crickets.

There is a bumper crop in the dust and weeds.
Coffee is drying on the ground, there are shells
       of corn, firewood.
Leather is curing out by the charcoals, the clothesline
needs repair, but no need to hurry:
       summer is several weeks away
       and a tax refund is in the mail.

Trinkets both charmed and disenchanted
lay scattered about: fossils, leaves,
quartz flakes, plastic pearls,
dusty paperbacks, an unfinished bookcase,
interplanetary debris, electrical wires,
opals, a toy solar system, a lost doll,
a broken aquarium, a rusted wagon.
       A self
that puts it all together somehow.
       Outside

we are building a fire. There is some food
and plenty of wood. Bring a bucket of beer,
some marshmallows, garlic cloves,
braids of trellising flowers, radishes,
gourds and pumpkins; it is nice

here in these hills, all high above

the edges of expressways,
          the sidewalks
of neighborhoods, higher than the tilt-
yards of churches, above the paths
of easy climbing. Up here

they have kept the Spanish missions,
preserved them for tourists, schoolchildren, history.
The grounds surrounding these pockmarked buildings
          are tranquil. Flowers,
          cats; red breasted
          robins parley themselves
through the subtle necessities of nature. Carousels,
someone wound them while we were out searching
for something to cook with. Where are the condiments?

Starry firmament, is it true that you are "ice cold"?
My thirst needs quenching under this sun.
Starry firmament … you look peaceful. Down here
we are engrossed with tamales and chiggers.
The jukebox is on. Now we are dancing.

And now, we have something to say
about first principles, about the contrast of colors,
          the cacophony of feather
trailing cirrus clouds (more ice in this coffee, please)
          about the topographic
features of vanishing points, and the act of acceptance.

Separated from sense content, ideas, like wine bubbles
are a kind of membrane, a kind of shell.
In the concept, there is a sense of evacuation, or rest.
But in the object there is always a filling
of demands, contracts. This is the nature of extension.
But really, they are most endearing when almost empty,
when they are holding only possibilities. See, they float:
parachutes, dandelions, soul wind, breath.
They are lifting into the blue, they are so light.

No Single Thought

I

No single thought had sent him drifting,
kicking empty bottles through a narrow
eyelet of crumbling sheetrock. Something

about the way each fissure, each filament
of a cluttered and debris covered incline
tangled into mysterious forms, had set
        him reaching,

had set him wandering the wet weeds,
had set him wondering about marks
he had read on a page, once, that said

"All things would be made new." Not
manifest now by these broken elements;
not found in the departure of his current
        landscape. Imagination

could not save him from the worrisome sun,
or influence the roll of old dice, or foretell
the judgment of sometimes bitter skies.

II

There at the lapping edge of a current,
where the dead grass turns a brittle shade,
there a message on the fence post read:

"There will be no chilling out
in the fires of hell," he thought
well phrased, but perhaps
        slightly joyless,

there an old tom, his grey fur patchy,
hunted for morsels, something to munch on,
something warm, with feathers and bright

blood, wet for his whiskers. Prowling
beneath a horned moon, in blooms
of hyacinth and prickly pear;
an uneasy marriage
between the unexpected and the commonplace.

III
Drifting, he settles in the dying light, symbols
falling about him like clapboard, picking
at his food, and sighing at the dimpled
wink of roses

that had found him out, at last. Her thorns
nestled in, all simple now, the texture
of desire, the quilt soft, and clean smelling,

smoothing the wrinkles of despair. His thoughts,
a patterned mosaic in time, press the springs
of remembrance and gratitude, echoing faintly,
like a hymn note.

He would give to whatever made this. A dream,
a reflective bliss, a passion for waters, swift
or motionless, fashioning, holding him now

like something known, an intercessor, a friend,
encircling him in the lights of embrace,
presenting him, and placing him somehow in,
new reunions.

迷路

About The Author

William Buck lives and writes in Austin, Texas. Contact him at williambuck@my.unt.edu.

www.ingramcontent.com/pod-product-compliance
Lightning Source LLC
Chambersburg PA
CBHW020509030426
42337CB00011B/309